Perfect
PUNCTUATION

SONIA MEHTA

PUFFIN BOOKS

An imprint of Penguin Random House

PUFFIN BOOKS

USA | Canada | UK | Ireland | Australia
New Zealand | India | South Africa | China | Singapore

Puffin Books is part of the Penguin Random House group of companies
whose addresses can be found at global.penguinrandomhouse.com

Published by Penguin Random House India Pvt. Ltd
4th Floor, Capital Tower 1, MG Road,
Gurugram 122 002, Haryana, India

First published in Puffin Books by Penguin Random House India 2018

Text, design and illustrations copyright © Quadrum Solutions Pvt. Ltd 2018
Series copyright © Penguin Random House India 2018

10 9 8 7 6 5 4 3 2

ISBN 9780143444909

Design and layout by Quadrum Solutions Pvt. Ltd

Printed at Repro India Limited

www.penguin.co.in

Dear MOMS and DADS

Over the years, I have discovered that the smartest, most confident kids, are those who have great language and communication skills. They are able to get their thoughts and ideas across in the most effective way, and this helps build their confidence.

And one of the best ways to help them develop these skills, is to give them a strong foundation. We recognize that English is a language that will remain important to them in their future lives—both professional and personal. Which is why, in the **Fun with English** series of books, we have focussed on bringing alive those aspects of the language that will add flair to children's communication when they speak or write.

English is a language that has many subtle nuances. The simplest sentence can be brought alive with an appropriate idiom, a well-chosen figure of speech or a colourful proverb. The correct use of punctuation and phonic sounds adds dramatically to the written or spoken word. By focussing creatively on all these, the **Fun with English** series aims to help kids get comfortable with some of the more confusing aspects of the language in a manner that is exciting and challenging.

I've enjoyed writing these books and I've re-discovered the joy of English as I did. I hope you enjoy these books with your children too.

SONIA MEHTA

Hello KIDS

Have you ever wondered why English has so many strange and interesting words and phrases in it? What does the proverb 'a stitch in time saves nine' mean? What do you picture when you hear the idiomatic expression 'it's raining cats and dogs'? What's the difference between a comma and an ellipsis? These are just some of the many things the **Fun with English** series will help you find out more about.

What's more, when you're done with the series, you'll be able to use idioms, figures of speech, proverbs, punctuation and phonics like a pro!

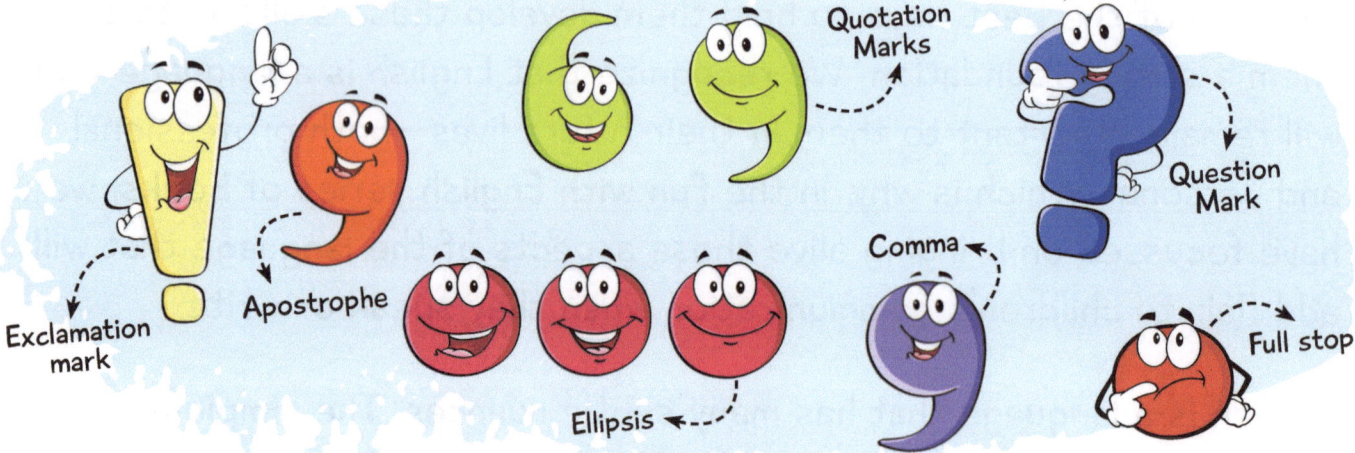

In the picture above, you'll see a whole bunch of familiar faces. These punctuation marks help to make what you write clearer.

There are many, many punctuation marks, but let's take a look at the most commonly used ones.

FULL STOP (.) This little mark tells your reader that a sentence is complete.
Merry Markle goes to the market.

COMMA (,) A comma tells you where there is a break in a sentence or a list.
Merry Markle went to the market, but she forgot her purse. (The comma is right between two phrases, both of which can be independent sentences by themselves. That's where a comma steps in. Remember, commas are also used to break a list. Commas are also used to separate items in a list. For example, *tea, coffee, bread and milk.*)

QUESTION MARK (?) This one is easy. It says you're asking a question.

Will you join Merry Markle when she goes to the market?

EXCLAMATION MARK (!) This little fellow tells your reader that you are excited.

Oh wow! Look at that mountain!

QUOTATION MARK (' ') These are always used in pairs and tell you when someone is speaking.

'Come with me,' Merry Markle said to Jolly Jenny.

ELLIPSIS (. . .) These three dots indicate an unfinished thought, a leading statement, a slight pause, an echoing voice, or a nervous or awkward silence.

Merry Markle thought to herself, 'I wonder whether there are cherries for sale yet . . .'

APOSTROPHE (') This little squiggle tells you when something belongs to someone.

That is Miss Markle's basket.

An apostrophe is also used to put two small words together. It replaces an alphabet.
It is a long walk to the market. It's a long walk to the market. (The letter i has been dropped and has been replaced with an apostrophe.)

CAPITAL LETTER You know of course that capital letters are used at the beginning of the name of a person, city, or country, that is, most proper nouns. The first word of a sentence also always begins with a capital letter.

Now that we've gone through some of the punctuation marks we use the most, let's have some fun with them.

So come along and let's jump right in. I hope you enjoy this book. I certainly had a blast writing it.

Lots of love,

SONIA AUNTY

PS: Do e-mail me if you have anything you'd like to say about this book.

sonia.mehta@quadrumltd.com

In the Right Place

Mr Verbose has said so many things, but these sentences seem to have no punctuation. Can you add the punctuation and rewrite these sentences?

1 Ouch that hurt

_____

2 Where have you hidden the gold

_____

3 I have eaten the apple

_____

4 Wow thats amazing

_____

5 What time shall we leave

_____

6 I love blue red green and pink

_____

7 Oh my what a pretty colour

_____

At Top Speed

Huffpuff talks so fast that he quite forgets to punctuate his sentences. Can you add punctuation marks to his message so that it makes sense?

the other day I went to watch a movie the name of the movie was star battles i ate three whole tubs of popcorn during the movie. While I was there I met poppy, my childhood friend oh my god it had been so long since i had last seen her I invited her to tea I said will you come have tea with me tomorrow

_____

_____

_____

_____

_____

_____

_____

HINT Add capital letters, quotation marks, commas, full stops and exclamation marks.

That's Capital!

Confused Connie has got a little mixed up here. Can you correct her capitalization? Circle the letters that are incorrectly capitalized and the ones that should be capitalized.

i went with jenny to the cinema.

The name of the movie was happy tails.

it was about a Dog named benji.

The family that Owned benji lived in london.

benji loved to Play in a park called hyde park.

One day, Benji dropped his ball in the lake.

His owner, a boy called jerry helped him get it out.

it was a great movie.

Super Blooper

Mrs Blooper has made some funny punctuation errors here. Tick (✔) the sentences below that are correctly punctuated.

- [ ] Hunters please use caution when hunting hikers. Use walking trails.

- [ ] Hunters. Please use caution when hunting hikers. Use walking trails.

- [ ] Hunters, please use caution when hunting. Hikers, use walking trails.

- [ ] Let's eat Grandma.

- [ ] Let's eat, Grandma.

- [ ] Go! Slow children crossing.

- [ ] Go slow! Children crossing.

End It Right!

The punctuation mark you use at the end of your sentence tells your reader a lot. Poor Miss Muffet has forgotten to end her sentences with punctuation marks. Can you add the right ones to each sentence below?

Hurry up

Do you want to miss the bus

It's a long drive to the next village

Oh dear

I have forgotten my purse

We will have to go back to get it

Now we will definitely miss the bus

What a bother

Will you be a dear and get

my purse for me

Punctuation Station

The names of the different punctuation marks are hidden in this grid. Can you find them all?

comma   full stop   exclamation mark   question mark

quotation mark   apostrophe   ellipsis

A	S	W	E	D	C	V	F	R	T	G	B	N	H	T
E	X	C	L	A	M	A	T	I	O	N	M	A	R	K
Z	A	S	X	C	D	F	V	B	G	H	N	N	H	U
A	W	S	E	E	L	L	I	P	S	I	S	U	I	O
Q	L	Q	U	E	S	T	I	O	N	M	A	R	K	L
Q	A	M	P	O	I	U	Y	T	R	E	W	Q	A	S
O	W	Y	A	P	O	S	T	R	O	P	H	E	T	C
L	C	O	M	M	A	V	B	N	H	G	T	Y	H	J
P	C	R	Y	U	I	F	U	L	L	S	T	O	P	E
X	D	Q	W	S	D	E	R	F	T	G	H	Y	U	N
Q	U	O	T	A	T	I	O	N	M	A	R	K	E	R

Oops!

Mrs Blooper is at it again. Can you rewrite her sentences to be grammatically correct?

1 Oh? I just love ice cream?

_____

2 Hey. You there. Stop at once.

_____

3 Oops. did i make the same mistake twice!

_____

4 Are you not coming for a walk with me.

_____

5 That dress is ghastly? Wouldn't you agree.

_____

6 Lets go quickly to the sale.

_____

The commas have gone on a rampage and are appearing in all the wrong places. Can you rewrite these sentences and put the commas in the right places?

Jenny Joe Jill and Jerry are off on a lovely, picnic, They are going to go to a meadow that has a lake, right next to it. There are plenty, of fish birds frogs and even crocodiles. Jenny, wants to chase butterflies but Jill would prefer, to sit, and eat cake sandwiches and chips.

_____

_____

_____

_____

_____

_____

Match Them Right

Matchmaker Mary is trying to get her punctuation right. She needs to match each statement to the right punctuation mark. Can you help?

Hey •  • ?

What is this •  • ,

Yes •  • !

Hi there, she said. •  •

Eggs beans and muffins •   •

Question Mark Maze

Questioning Quentin loves mazes. He is trying to find his way out of this maze by following the sentences that are questions. Can you help him along?

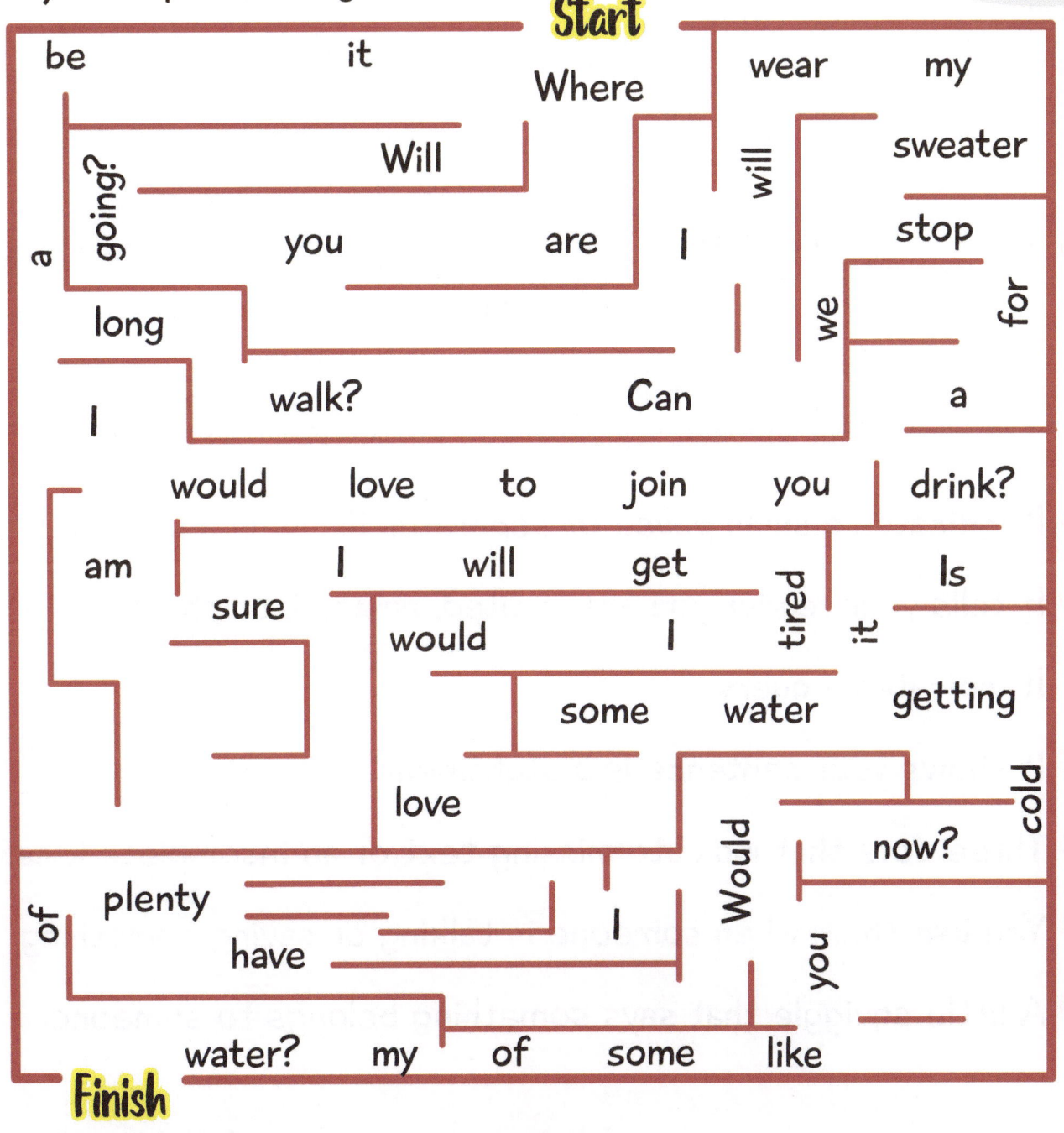

Start

be   it
              Where
        Will
a   going?
        you   are   I
  long
                walk?   Can
I
    would   love   to   join   you   drink?
am   I   will   get   Is
    sure
        would   I
            some   water   getting
        love
of plenty   Would   now?   cold
    have   I   you
    water?   my   of   some   like

wear   my
            sweater
will   stop
        we   for
                a

tired   it

Finish

13

Punctuation Quiz

Punctuation Pam has devised a word quiz to check if you know your punctuation. Want to try it? Simply solve with the help of clues.

1.			M												
2.				M											
3.									R						
4.					P										
5.			P												
6.				O											
7.			R												

1 It indicates a small pause or separates items in a list.

2 It tells your reader you are excited, amazed, or shocked.

3 It indicates a query.

4 It shows your sentence is a statement.

5 Three dots that indicate missing text or an incomplete idea.

6 You use them when someone is talking or saying something.

7 A little squiggle that says something belongs to someone.

Punctuation Path

Miss Markle has something to say. Can you colour the path that ends in a question mark and then write the sentence below?

Start

will	glass	join	arrive	when
you	come	she	go	also
computer	to	my	see	here
me	please	house	which	now
happy	refuse	for	dinner	tomorrow
sweet	sure	please	never	?

Finish

_____

_____

Nonsense Message

Jumbledore has sent a message to his friend. But his friend can't make sense of it because Jumbledore seems to have forgotten to use punctuation. Can you help him make sense of it by adding punctuation wherever it is missing? Then write the paragraph out in the space below.

tomorrow is larrys birthday I would love to throw a party for him it is a sunday we can make a cake with eggs flour butter and chocolate I started to make the cake but ate all the chocolate can you send some chocolate over to my house please

Punctuation Potpourri

Hotchpotch has mixed up a whole lot of things into her punctuation potpourri. Can you help her unscramble the words below? Remember, the clue is in the punctuation mark.

1 CHUO _____

2 OHW YNMA _____ _____

3 KOYA _____ I agree.

4 OLOK HEERT _____ _____ she

said, pointing at the sky.

5 REA UOY RSUE _____

_____

Hide 'N' Seek

Hidden in this word grid are six words that should have a punctuation mark after them. Can you find those words and then write them with the correct punctuation marks?

W	O	W	E	R	T	Y	U	I	Y	E	S	W	Q
Q	A	W	S	E	D	R	F	T	G	Y	H	U	J	I
A	Z	S	X	W	H	A	T	R	T	Y	I	K	E	S
Z	A	X	S	C	D	V	F	B	G	H	N	J	M	K
A	S	D	F	G	H	J	K	W	H	E	N	W	E	R
Z	X	N	O	A	S	W	E	D	R	F	T	G	Y	H

_____ _____ _____

_____ _____ _____

Question Maze ?

Lost Larry is trying to get out of the maze by following those words that need a question mark at the end. Can you help him?

sit
bye
yes
look
what
there
never
hello
here
okay
who
no
Finish
some
Start
where
why
when
how much
which
what if
me
now
ever
you
come

Clue Cracker

Snoopy Sam is good at solving word puzzles. But his punctuation is a bit rusty. Can you help him find the phrase below that needs an exclamation mark at the end?

I = 10   A = 8   E = 5
G = 1   O = 2   D = 3
N = 4   S = 6   R = 7
C = 9   U = 12   M = 11

1 2 2 3 4 5 6 6

1 7 8 9 10 2 12 6

11 5

Barrel of Fun

Match the barrels to the correct punctuation marks.

Eww

Sure

How

Bread butter and jam

Go away, she said.

Lost Luggage

Circle the letters that are incorrectly capitalized below.

jo and janet were best Friends.

One day they Went to japan together.

they took the orient express on thursday.

sadly they lost their Luggage.

they complained TO the ticket master.

their luggage was no where to be found.

They called home and found
that they had Forgotten
their Bags at home.

Who does that?

Crack the Code

Detective Dan is on the prowl. Here he's trying to crack the coded message to find a question. Can you find it too?

A = 5   D = 10   E = 9   H = 1   I = 15   L = 13   O = 6
R = 7   U = 0   V = 17   W = 4   Y = 2

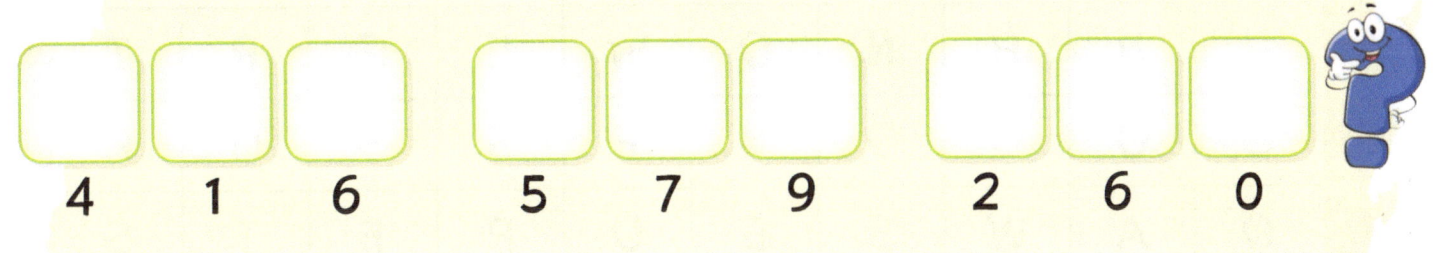

4 1 6   5 7 9   2 6 0

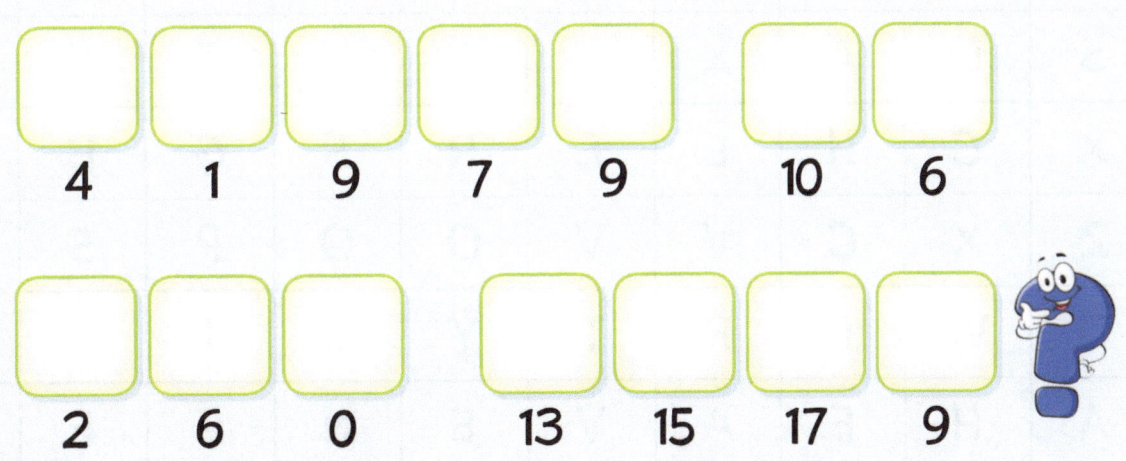

4 1 9 7 9   10 6

2 6 0   13 15 17 9

23

Exclamation Word Search!

Excitable Ella uses eight words all the time. Can you find them in this word grid? Remember, they are all end in exclamation marks.

Q	A	W	S	E	D	R	W	O	W
E	E	U	G	H	H	G	H	J	K
Z	J	K	X	C	D	F	V	B	G
H	N	H	N	Q	W	E	G	R	T
G	O	O	D	N	E	S	S	G	H
Q	A	W	S	E	D	R	F	T	G
Y	H	E	Y	T	G	Y	H	U	J
W	Q	G	O	S	H	B	N	M	B
S	D	A	X	X	C	V	T	N	M
X	C	H	E	E	R	S	G	B	M
Z	X	C	V	V	O	O	P	S	R
Q	W	E	R	T	Y	U	I	B	N
A	H	E	A	V	E	N	S	E	B

Missed!

Old Mr Moony keeps forgetting to punctuate his sentences. Can you help him out? Rewrite these sentences using the correct punctuation marks.

1 Oh dear I seem to have lost my spectacles again

_____

2 I asked mrs moony to help me look for them

_____

3 we looked under the mat in the cupboard and even in the refrigerator

_____

4 just go to sleep she said to me

_____

5 but I can't sleep without reading for a bit

_____

6 I went to brush my teeth and do you know what I found in the mug

_____

Merry Maze

Lost Larry is lost again. This time he needs to find the way out by using words that need exclamation marks after them.

Start

smile   garden

pencil   cheers   picnic

heavens

ouch   cup

goodness

game   hey   happy

party

sing   gosh

den

wow   oops   rubbish

pop   huff

pot   puff

Finish

Unscramble Ramble

Jumbledore is now trying his best to unscramble these words. The clues are in the punctuation. Can you help?

1 PLHE ❗ _____ ❗

2 HNEW ❓ _____ ❓

3 RHEE 🔴 _____ 🔴

4 🟢 YEB YEB 🟢 _____ _____ 🟣 she

said to her friend.

5 AYY ❗ _____ ❗

6 OHW ❓ _____ ❓

7 AYMEB 🔴 _____ 🔴

All Jumbled Up

Jumble Joe loves word jumbles. Can you unscramble the words below and then add the right punctuation to each word?

A V H S E E N

_____

H H W I C

_____

R A I C E Y T N L

_____

That's a Statement. Full Stop!

This maze has got Smarty Sam confused. He needs to get out of it by following the sentences that are statements and have full stops at the end. Can you help him out?

Start

Finish

29

Mixed-up Message

Mixed-up Martha is writing a letter to her sister about her garden patch. But she seems to have neglected to add any punctuation. Can you add the right punctuation marks and rewrite her letter below?

dear mary

i am so worried about my garden yesterday jimmy the gardener came and checked the roses dahlias lilies and violets they all seem to have wilted the problem is the rain we have had no rainfall for so long we must water the plants well I told jimmy but he will not listen I am at my wits end what do you think I should do

_____

_____

_____

_____

_____

_____

_____

Pathfinder

Hiker Horace is always discovering new paths. He's found a path that makes a statement and ends with a full stop. Can you follow the path and find the statement too?

Start

The	an	hen	pig	run	door	black
naughty	a	fox	bear	sock	table	net
brown	fox	growled	glow	arm	bottle	fish
smart	hardly	at	them	picnic	water	pool
clever	smiling	the	dog	window	drink	watch
snoring	some	owl	who	was	giggling	smile
sweet	sun	howled	grin	asleep	in	show
lovely	rain	shimmer	shape	freeze	the	kennel

Finish

31

The Question Garden

Can you match each question word to the flower that has the answers in the petals?

Who?   What?   When?   Where?
        How many?   How often?

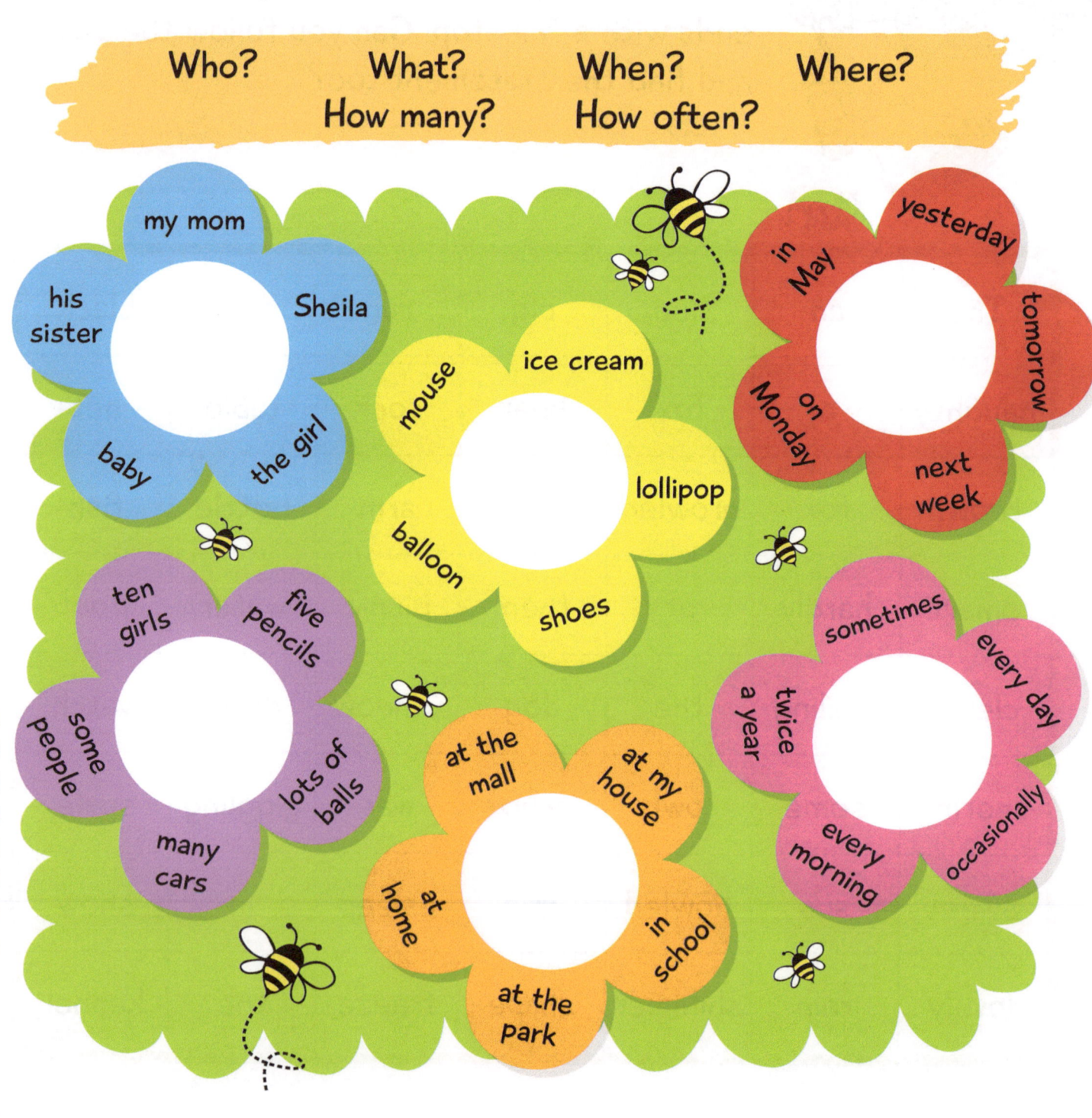

my mom
his sister
Sheila
baby
the girl

mouse
ice cream
lollipop
balloon
shoes

in May
yesterday
tomorrow
on Monday
next week

ten girls
five pencils
some people
lots of balls
many cars

at the mall
at my house
at home
in school
at the park

sometimes
every day
twice a year
occasionally
every morning

32

Unjumble Time

Jumbledore has solved this puzzle and is now trying to get his friends to solve it too. Can you? Remember, the clue is in the punctuation.

1 LEWL NDOE _____ _____

2 HHWCI _____

3 FO OSRUEC _____ _____

4 OCEM RHEE _____ _____

the teacher said, beckoning the student to

her side.

5 ALELRY _____

Follow the Path

Eager Emily is always exclaiming something or other. Can you find out what she's trying to say? Follow the words that make a sentence with an exclamation mark at the end.

Start

what	sunrise	amazing	really	everyday
a	truly	wow	bright	sometimes
computer	wonderful	sight	strong	evening
morning	moonlight	the	rising	meadow
stars	earth	golden	sunset	is
twinkle	mud	ground	hill	!

Finish

What's Wrong

Mrs Blooper is making new mistakes. Tick (✔) the sentences below that are correctly punctuated.

☐ I ate my cat. Is still hungry. So I gave her some milk.

☐ I ate my cat is still hungry so I gave her some milk

☐ I ate. My cat is still hungry, so I gave her some milk.

☐ My granny experiences difficulty eating she tires easily

☐ My granny experiences difficulty eating. She tires easily.

☐ My granny. Experiences difficulty. Eating she tires easily.

☐ Jenny loves cooking her family and her dog.

☐ Jenny loves cooking, her family and her dog.

☐ Jenny loves cooking. Her family and her dog.

Clue Flu

Puzzled Peter is feverishly trying to crack this mystery. He needs to find words that end with the punctuation marks shown below. Can you help him out?

A = 4   M = 3   Z = 1   N = 2   G = 8   I = 9

4   3   4   1   9   2   8

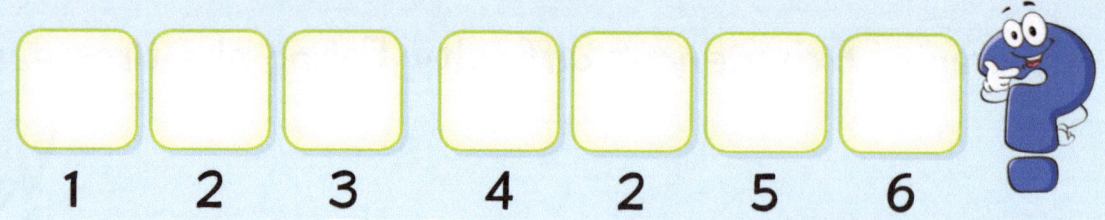

H = 1   O = 2   W = 3   C = 4   M = 5   E = 6

1   2   3   4   2   5   6

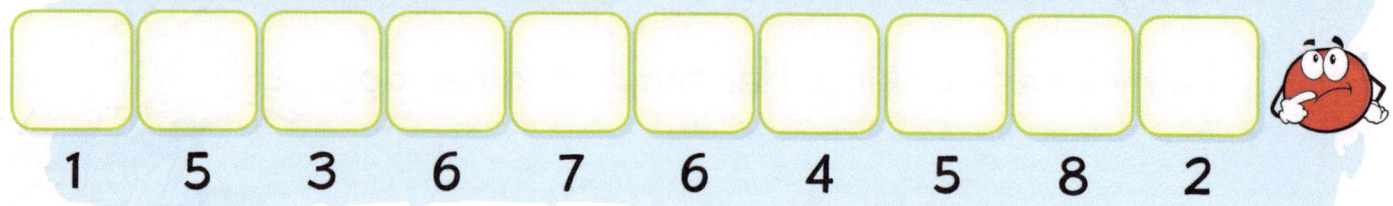

E = 5   D = 1   I = 6   F = 3   N = 7   T = 4   L = 8   Y = 2

1   5   3   6   7   6   4   5   8   2

Match Catch

Timmy and Tammy are racing to see who will match the left and right columns correctly first. Want to join the race?

Yes •

Fantastic •

Oh really •

Right,
he said •

Trees bushes
and flowers •

Lost in Questions?

Curious Cate is full of questions. She has gotten lost in a maze of them. Can you follow all the sentences that are questions and help Cate out of the maze?

reptiles
animals
trees
forest
cackle
they
cat?
mammals
hen
Are
the
den
hen
live?
a
What
weep
lions
Is
Finish
lions?
Start
egg
lion
a
clouds
do
Where
howl
loud
biggest
fox
are
jungle
colour
animals?
is
wind
How
barn
What
roar?
Why
their

What's Odd?

Finicky Fred can see that one word doesn't belong in each row below. Can you find it? Place the right punctuation mark next to each word, and then circle the odd word out.

why ☐   what ☐   yes ☐   when ☐   who ☐

wow ☐   yay ☐   anytime ☐   super ☐   gosh ☐

yes ☐   sure ☐   mine ☐   where ☐   come ☐

oh really ☐   of course ☐   gosh ☐   whose ☐

heavens ☐   my goodness ☐   perhaps ☐   ouch ☐

Find Your Way

Can you find your way out of this maze by following all the words that should start with capital letters? Colour those letters to mark the path.

Start

london	theatre	play	clock	mouse	switch	end
paris	mumbai	school	curtain	cow	fan	start
ground	geoffery	mall	funny	glass	grandpa	jump
silly	nasik	maya	joe	table	wall	swim
girl	uncle	song	sunday	january	picture	leap
boy	aunt	rock	laugh	tokyo	april	gargle
woman	watch	band	cry	painting	jupiter	finland

Finish

Hidden Marks

Can you find six punctuation marks hidden in this picture?

GOOD MORNING

milk

NICE DAY

ABC

#1

LIVING TO THE FULLEST

Paper Blooper

Mr Know-a-Lot simply can't understand the news today. Can you help him by adding the punctuation marks and rewriting the news for him?

DOG CROSSES. TRACK STOPS TRAIN

In a strange incident today a dog crossed a track and stopped a train bobo the dog is a trained police dog he was looking for some thieves he must have smelled something on the tracks he sniffed among the stones trees and bushes what can you smell bobo his handler asked him but he simply sat on the tracks the train was forced to stop

_____

_____

_____

_____

_____

_____

Hotch-Potch Tea Invite

Jumbledore is at it again. This time he has got his words right, but the order of the words in his sentences is wrong. Can you put the words in the right order and rewrite each sentence? Remember to add punctuation in the right places too.

1 tea am some making am i

_____

2 me you like would join to

_____

3 hot the is teapot out watch

_____

4 cake have too sandwiches I cookies apple pie and

_____

_____

5 fun it don't be think you will

_____

ANSWERS

Page 4 In the Right Place
1. Ouch! That hurt.; 2. Where have you hidden the gold?;
3. I have eaten the apple.; 4. Wow! That's amazing.; 5. What time shall we leave?; 6. I love blue, red, green and pink.; 7. Oh my, what a pretty colour!

Page 5 At Top Speed
The other day, I went to watch a movie. The name of the movie was Star Battles. I ate three whole tubs of popcorn during the movie. While I was there, I met Poppy, my childhood friend. Oh my god! It had been so long since I had last seen her! I said, 'Will you come have tea with me tomorrow?'

Page 6 That's Capital!
Ⓘ went with Ⓙenny to the cinema.
The name of the movie was Ⓗappy Ⓣails.
Ⓘt was about a Ⓓog named Ⓑenji.
The family that Ⓞwned benji lived in Ⓛondon.
Ⓑenji loved to Ⓟlay in a park called Ⓗyde park.
One day, Benji dropped his ball in the lake.
His owner, a boy called Ⓙerry helped him get it out.
Ⓘt was a great movie.

Page 7 Super Blooper
Hunters, please use caution when hunting. Hikers, use walking trails.; Let's eat, Grandma.; Go slow! Children crossing.

Page 8 End It Right!
Hurry up! Do you want to miss the bus? It's a long drive to the next village. Oh dear! I have forgotten my purse. We will have to go back to get it. Now we will definitely miss the bus. What a bother! Will you be a dear and get my purse for me?

Page 9 Punctuation Station

A	S	W	E	D	C	V	F	R	T	G	B	N	H	T
E	X	C	L	A	M	A	T	I	O	N	M	A	R	K
Z	A	S	X	C	D	F	V	B	G	H	N	N	H	U
A	W	S	E	E	L	L	I	P	S	I	S	U	I	O
Q	L	Q	U	E	S	T	I	O	N	M	A	R	K	L
Q	A	M	P	O	I	U	Y	T	R	E	W	Q	A	S
O	W	Y	A	P	O	S	T	R	O	P	H	E	T	C
L	C	O	M	M	A	V	B	N	H	G	T	Y	H	J
P	C	R	Y	U	I	F	U	L	L	S	T	O	P	E
X	D	Q	W	S	D	E	R	F	T	G	H	Y	U	N
Q	U	O	T	A	T	I	O	N	M	A	R	K	E	R

Page 10 Oops!
1. Oh! I just love ice cream!; 2. Hey! You there! Stop at once!
3. Oops! Did I make the same mistake twice?; 4. Are you not

coming for a walk with me?; 5. That dress is ghastly! Wouldn't you agree?; 6. Let's go to the sale quickly.

Page 11 Comma Rampage
Jenny, Joe, Jill and Jerry are off on a lovely picnic. They are going to go to a meadow that has a lake right next to it. There are plenty of fish, birds, frogs and even crocodiles. Jenny wants to chase butterflies, but Jill would prefer to sit and eat cake, sandwiches and chips.

Page 12 Match Them Right
Hey—! (exclamation mark); What is this—? (question mark); Yes—. (full stop); Hi there, she said.—` ' (quotation marks); Eggs beans and muffins—, (comma)

Page 13 Question Mark Maze

Page 14 Punctuation Quiz
1. COMMA; 2. EXCLAMATION MARK; 3. QUESTION MARK;
4. FULL STOP; 5. ELLIPSIS; 6. QUOTATION MARKS;
7. APOSTROPHE

Page 15 Punctuation Path

will	glass	join	arrive	when
you	come	she	go	also
computer	to	my	see	here
me	please	house	which	now
happy	refuse	for	dinner	tomorrow
sweet	sure	please	never	?

Ans: Will you come to my house for dinner tomorrow?

Page 16 Nonsense Message
Tomorrow is Larry's birthday. I would love to throw a party for him. It is a Sunday. We can make a cake with eggs, flour, butter and chocolate. I started to make the cake, but ate all the chocolate. Can you send some chocolate over to my house, please?

Page 17 Punctuation Potpourri
1. Ouch!; 2. How many?; 3. Okay.; 4. `Look there,'; 5. Are you sure?

Page 18 Hide 'N' Seek

W	O	W	W	E	R	T	Y	U	I	Y	E	S	W	Q
Q	A	W	S	E	D	R	F	T	G	Y	H	U	J	I
A	Z	S	X	W	H	A	T	R	T	Y	I	K	E	S
Z	A	X	S	C	D	V	F	B	G	H	N	J	M	K
A	S	D	F	G	H	J	K	W	H	E	N	W	E	R
Z	X	N	O	A	S	W	E	D	R	F	T	G	Y	H

WOW!; YES.; WHAT?; YIKES!; WHEN?; NO.

Page 19 Question Maze

Page 20 Clue Cracker
GOODNESS GRACIOUS ME!

Page 21 Barrel of Fun
Eww—! (exclamation mark); Sure—. (full stop); How—?
(question mark); Bread butter and jam—, (comma); Go away,
she said.—` ' (quotation marks)

Page 22 Lost Luggage
(J)o and (j)anet were the best (F)riends.
One day they (W)ent to (j)apan together.
(t)hey took the (o)rient express on (t)hursday.
(s)adly they lost their (L)uggage.
(t)hey complained (TO) the ticket master.
(t)heir luggage was nowhere to be found.
They called home and found that they had (F)orgotten their (B)ags
at home.
Who does that?

Page 23 Crack the Code
WHO ARE YOU?; WHERE DO YOU LIVE?

Page 24 Exclamation Word Search

Q	A	W	S	E	D	R	W	O	W
E	E	U	G	H	H	G	H	J	K
Z	J	K	X	C	D	F	V	B	G
H	N	H	N	Q	W	E	G	R	T
G	O	O	D	N	E	S	S	G	H
Q	A	W	S	E	D	R	F	T	G
Y	H	E	Y	T	G	Y	H	U	J
W	Q	G	O	S	H	B	N	M	B
S	D	A	X	X	C	V	M	N	M
X	C	H	E	E	R	S	G	B	M
Z	X	C	V	V	O	O	P	S	P
Q	W	E	R	T	Y	U	I	E	B
A	H	E	A	V	E	N	S	E	B

Page 25 Missed!
1. Oh dear! I seem to have lost my spectacles again.; 2. I asked
Mrs Moony to help me look for them.; 3. We looked under the
mat, in the cupboard and even in the refrigerator.; 4. 'Just go
to sleep,' she said to me.; 5. But I can't sleep without reading
for a bit.; 6. I went to brush my teeth and do you know what I
found in the mug?

Page 26 Merry Maze

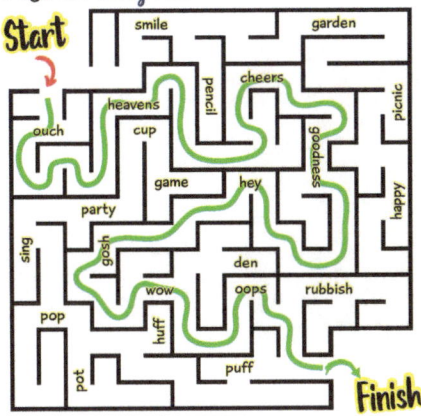

Page 27 Unscramble Ramble
1. Help!; 2. When?; 3. Here.; 4. 'Bye bye'; 5. Yay!; 6. Who?;
7. Sure.

Page 28 Riddle-Dee-Dee
HEAVENS!; WHICH?; CERTAINLY.

Page 29 That's a Statement. Full Stop!

Page 30 Mixed-up Message
Dear Mary,

I am so worried about my garden. Yesterday, Jimmy the
gardener came and checked the roses, dahlias, lilies and violets.
They all seem to have wilted. The problem is the rain. We have
had no rainfall for so long. 'We must water the plants well,' I
told Jimmy, but he will not listen. I am at my wits' end! What do
you think I should do?

Page 31 Pathfinder

The	an	hen	pig	run	door	black
naughty	a	fox	bear	sock	table	net
brown	fox	growled	glow	arm	bottle	fish
smart	hardly	at	them	picnic	water	pool
clever	smiling	the	dog	window	drink	watch
snoring	some	owl	who	was	giggling	smile
sweet	sun	howled	grin	asleep	in	show
lovely	rain	shimmer	shape	freeze	the	kennel

Page 32 The Question Garden

Page 33 Unjumble Time

1. Well done!; 2. Which?; 3. Of course.; 4. 'Come here'; 5. Really?

Page 34 Follow the Path

what	sunrise	amazing	really	everyday
a	truly	wow	bright	sometimes
computer	wonderful	sight	strong	evening
morning	moonlight	the	rising	meadow
stars	earth	golden	sunset	is
twinkle	mud	ground	hill	

What a truly wonderful sight the golden sunset is!

Page 35 What's Wrong?

I ate. My cat is still hungry, so I gave her some milk.; My granny experiences difficulty eating. She tires easily.; Jenny loves cooking, her family and her dog.

Page 36 Clue Flue

AMAZING!; HOW COME?; DEFINITELY.

Page 37 Match Catch

Yes—. (full stop); Fantastic—! (exclamation mark); Oh really—? (question mark); Right, he said—" (quotation marks); Trees bushes and flowers—, (comma)

Page 38 Lost in Questions

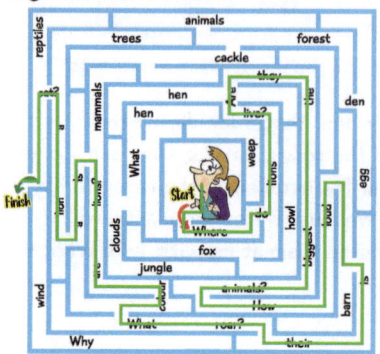

Page 39 What's Odd?

yes; anytime; where; whose; perhaps

Page 40 Find Your Way

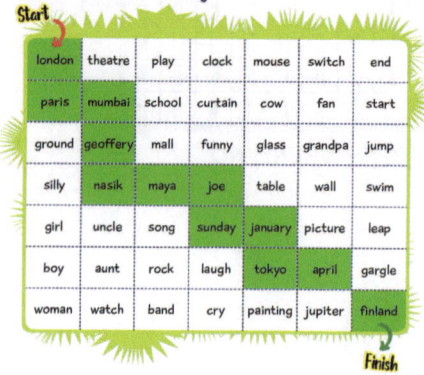

london	theatre	play	clock	mouse	switch	end
paris	mumbai	school	curtain	cow	fan	start
ground	geoffery	mall	funny	glass	grandpa	jump
silly	nasik	maya	joe	table	wall	swim
girl	uncle	song	sunday	january	picture	leap
boy	aunt	rock	laugh	tokyo	april	gargle
woman	watch	band	cry	painting	jupiter	finland

Page 41 Hidden Marks

Page 42 Paper Blooper

DOG CROSSES TRACK, STOPS TRAIN

In a strange incident, today, a dog crossed a track and stopped a train. Bobo the dog is a trained police dog. He was looking for some thieves. He must have smelled something on the tracks. He sniffed among the stones, trees and bushes. 'What can you smell, Bobo?' his handler asked him, but he simply sat on the tracks. The train was forced to stop.

Page 43 Hotch-Potch Tea Invite

1. I am making some tea.; 2. Would you like to join me?; 3. Watch out! The teapot is hot.; 4. I have sandwiches, cookies, apple pie and cake too.; 5. Don't you think it will be fun?